ROME

NEEDS YOU!

- EMPERORS • CHARIOTEERS •
- LEGIONARIES • VESTAL VIRGINS •
- SLAVES • MERCHANTS •
- GLADIATORS • INNKEEPERS •
- SOOTHSAYERS • MOSAIC MAKERS •
- LAWYERS •

AND MANY MORE JOBS AVAILABLE
APPLY AT THE FORUM

Library of Congress Cataloging-in-Publication Data

Ganeri, Anita, 1961-
  Emperors and gladiators / Anita Ganeri.
    p. cm. – (All in a day's work)
  Originally published: Great Britain : David West children's books, 1997.
  ISBN 0-87226-661-3
  1. Rome--Social life and customs–Juvenile literature. 2. Social
classes–Rome–Juvenile literature. 3. Occupations–Rome–Juvenile literature. [1.
Rome–Social life and customs.] I. Title. II Series.

  DG78 .G373 2001
  305.5'0945'63-dc21

First published in the United States in 2001 by
Peter Bedrick Books
A division of NTC/Contemporary Publishing Group, Inc.
4255 West Touhy Avenue, Lincolnwood (Chicago),
Illinois 60712 - 1975 U.S.A.
Copyright © 1997 David West Children's Books
Text copyright © 1997 Anita Ganeri

Consultant: Dr Simon James
Illustrators: Simone Boni, Roger Stewart (Virgil Pomfret
Agency), Francis Phillips, Ken Stott (B.L. Kearley Ltd)

Designed and produced in Great Britain by
David West 𐀀𐀀 Children's Books,
7 Princeton Court, 55 Felsham Road, London SW15 1AZ

First published in Great Britain in 1997 by
Heinemann Children's Reference, an imprint of
Heinemann Educational Publishers, Halley Court,
Jordan Hill, Oxford OX2 8EJ, a division of Reed
Educational and Professional Publishing Limited.

Printed in Italy.
International Standard Book Number: 0-87226-661-3
10 9 8 7 6 5 4 3 2 1

ALL · IN · A · DAY'S · WORK

EMPERORs
AND
GLADIATORS

ANITA GANERI

PETER BEDRICK BOOKS

NTC/Contemporary Publishing Group

CONTENTS

THE PAGE NUMBERS IN THIS BOOK ARE IN ROMAN NUMERALS. HERE'S HOW THEY TRANSLATE:

1 I	12 XII	23 XXIII	34 XXXIV
2 II	13 XIII	24 XXIV	35 XXXV
3 III	14 XIV	25 XXV	36 XXXVI
4 IV	15 XV	26 XXVI	37 XXXVII
5 V	16 XVI	27 XXVII	38 XXXVIII
6 VI	17 XVII	28 XXVIII	39 XXXIX
7 VII	18 XVIII	29 XXIX	40 XL
8 VIII	19 XIX	30 XXX	50 L
9 IX	20 XX	31 XXXI	100 C
10 X	21 XXI	32 XXXII	500 D
11 XI	22 XXII	33 XXXIII	1000 M

INTRODUCTION

Welcome to Ancient Rome! You've gone back in time almost 2,000 years to the capital of the Roman Empire. It's full of people going about their daily work. Discover the jobs they did, from slave to mighty Emperor. Your job depended a lot on whether you were rich or poor. If you were poor, you worked hard, perhaps as a craftworker or a shopkeeper. Life was easier if you were rich. You might have been a lawyer or a politician.

Will you find the job for you?

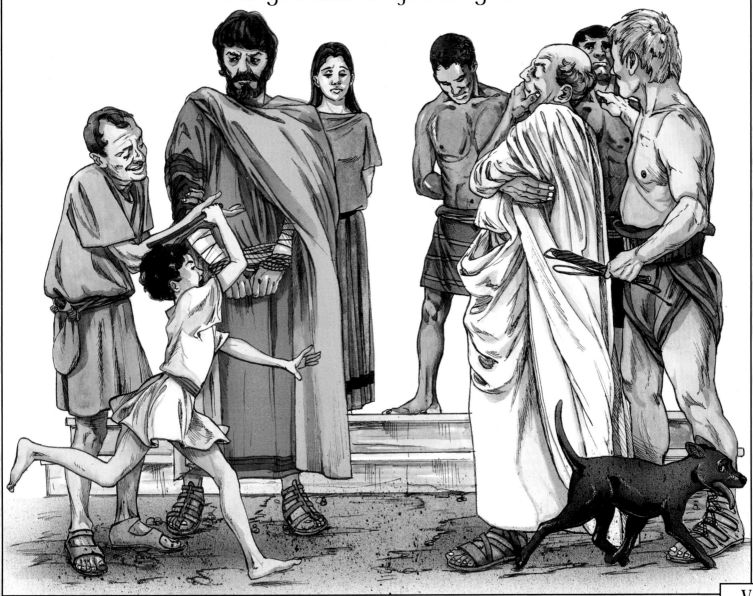

THE TOP JOB IN ANCIENT ROME was that of Emperor. There were lots of perks. You were the most powerful person in Rome and in charge of a great empire. You got to live in a grand palace and had your head stamped on coins. You might have a triumphal arch built in your honor.

Triumphal arch

Your best chance of getting the job was to be adopted by the present Emperor. Then you succeeded to the throne when he died.

THE ROMAN

ROME •

EMPEROR AUGUSTUS

FULL NAME: Caius Julius Caesar Octavianus

OFFICIAL NAME: Augustus ("Revered One")

DATE OF BIRTH: 63BC

FAMILY: Adopted son of Julius Caesar. Married to Livia. One stepson, Tiberius (also his heir).

DISTINGUISHING FEATURES: Thought to be very handsome.

OCCUPATION: First Emperor of Rome (27BC-AD14); Chief Priest (Pontifex Maximus).

ACHIEVEMENTS: Brilliant politician. Wise and just. Made Rome prosperous and peaceful. Organized Rome's first fire brigade. An all-around great leader. Proclaimed a god after his death. The month Sextilis was renamed August in his honor.

On the other hand, you made many enemies and ran the risk of being assassinated. (Even poisoned by one of your family – it did happen!) You had to go off and fight in plenty of wars, for the sake of your reputation. And you never knew what you'd come home to.

EMPIRE

Three Emperors
Of course, not all Emperors were great like Augustus. Some were downright bad, or even mad.

CALIGULA (AD37-41)
CLAIMED TO BE A GOD AND HAD HIS HORSE MADE A SENATOR. MARRIED HIS SISTER AND LATER MURDERED HER. CRUEL AND EXTRAVAGANT.

VERDICT: COMPLETELY MAD.

CLAUDIUS (AD41-54)
FRAIL AND NERVOUS. HID IN A CUPBOARD WHEN CALIGULA WAS MURDERED BUT WAS LATER MADE EMPEROR.

VERDICT: NOT AS STUPID AS HE LOOKED. HE EXTENDED THE EMPIRE AND REFORMED THE CIVIL SERVICE.

NERO (AD54-68)
CLAUDIUS'S STEPSON. BEGAN WELL BUT SOON BECAME A BRUTAL TYRANT. MURDERED HIS MOTHER, WIFE, CLAUDIUS'S SON, BRITANNICUS, AND MANY OTHERS. SAID TO HAVE PLAYED THE FIDDLE WHILE HE WATCHED ROME BURN IN AD64.

VERDICT: MAD, BAD, AND DANGEROUS.

DID YOU KNOW?
Only the Emperor was allowed to wear an all-purple toga. Anyone else was guilty of high treason. The precious purple dye came from a type of seashell.

> **LAWYER REQUIRED TO DEFEND INNKEEPER AGAINST CHARGES OF FOOD POISONING.**
>
> •
>
> DIDIUS MAXIMUS
> THE JOLLY ROMAN
> NEAR THE FORUM

IF YOU COULD SPEAK WELL IN PUBLIC and argue your case, you might have become a lawyer. (A wealthy family and lots of confidence helped too!) Part of your training was with a special teacher who taught you how to use different tones of voice and gestures to get the jury on your side.

Trials were held in huge buildings, called basilicas. Anyone could accuse a person of a crime and force them to appear in court. You were hired to defend them. Everyone spoke, then the jury voted on whether the accused person was guilty or innocent, and the judge would decide on the punishment.

DID YOU KNOW?

To put burglars off, many rich Romans kept guard dogs. If you didn't want a dog, you could always have a mosaic, saying CAVE CANEM – Beware of the Dog – instead!

The accused might try to look sad or scruffy in court, to make the jury feel sorry for him!

JOB DESCRIPTION: GREAT PROSPECTS IN UP-AND-COMING PROFESSION.

PAY: COULD GET RICH WITH OPTIONAL EXTRAS FROM GRATEFUL CLIENTS.

In serious cases, there might be as many as 75 people on the jury.

If, on the other hand, you fell in with a bad lot and became a criminal, and you got caught, there were various punishments in store. You weren't sent to prison but...

...YOU COULD BE SENT TO WORK IN THE MINES, WHERE YOU MIGHT NOT LIVE LONG.

...YOU MIGHT BE EXILED AND LOSE YOUR ROMAN CITIZENSHIP.

...YOU MIGHT BE CRUCIFIED ON A WOODEN CROSS.

... IF YOU DESERTED FROM THE ARMY, YOU WERE STONED OR BEATEN TO DEATH BY YOUR COMRADES.

... IF YOU KILLED YOUR FATHER, YOU WERE PUT IN A SACK WITH A LIVE VIPER, COCKEREL, AND DOG AND THROWN IN A RIVER!

TICKETS TO THE GLADIATOR FIGHTS AT THE COLOSSEUM AT THE KNOCK-DOWN PRICE OF HALF A LIFETIME.

•

APPLY TO CHIEF PRIESTESS AT THE TEMPLE OF VESTA.

THERE WEREN'T MANY JOBS FOR GIRLS in Ancient Rome. They were expected to stay at home and look after the house. If you were really lucky, and from a good family, you might be asked to become a Vestal Virgin.

You had to leave home at about eight years old. Your hair was cut and hung on a tree outside the Temple of Vesta. The temple became your home for 30 years.

Your main duty was to guard the sacred fire inside the temple. Woe betide you if it ever went out. You also promised not to get married until the 30 years were up. (If anyone would have you then, that is. Most Roman girls were married at 14!) Of course, there were perks. To be picked at all was a very great honor, and you got a ring-side seat at gladiator fights in the Colosseum.

Vesta was the goddess of hearth and home. Her temple was in the Forum (market place), right in the center of Rome. Inside, a fire was kept burning in her honor. It was only allowed to go out on one day of the year – March 1, New Year's Day.

X

JOB DESCRIPTION: ONLY FOR GIRLS FROM GOOD FAMILIES. FREE FIRST-CLASS ACCOMMODATION IN CITY CENTER.

PAY: NONE. YOU DO IT FOR THE HONOR.

The festival of Vestalia on June 9 was a big day for Vestal Virgins. People came to the temple with gifts of food for the goddess. In return, you had to bake bread for the whole city while the bakers had the day off!

DID YOU KNOW?

If you broke your promise about getting married you were buried alive and left to starve to death! If you were lucky, a kind friend or relation might help you to escape.

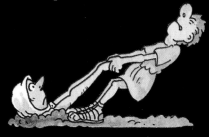

EXPANDING EMPIRE REQUIRES
ADVENTUROUS MERCHANTS.

FOREIGN LANGUAGE AND
MONEY SKILLS ESSENTIAL.
•
APPLY AT THE FORUM.

IF YOU WERE GOOD WITH NUMBERS and fond of adventure, the life of a merchant might be for you. The many newly built roads allowed merchants to trade and travel far and wide. They also traveled by sea, hiring sailing ships to carry their cargo.

Many merchants sailed with their cargoes to make sure they weren't stolen and that they got a good price. If you did travel by sea, there were several points to remember. (See page XIII.)

DID YOU KNOW?
Special officials checked the merchants' weights and measures to make quite sure their customers weren't being cheated or shortchanged.

JOB DESCRIPTION: WHEELING AND DEALING. WITH OPPORTUNITIES FOR FOREIGN TRAVEL.

PAY: IF YOU TAKE RISKS, YOU COULD MAKE A FORTUNE.

Every day, merchant ships left the bustling port of Ostia near Rome, loaded with goods. As they left, others arrived, bringing wheat from Egypt, olive oil and wine from Spain, wild animals from Africa, silk from China, wool from Britain, spices from India, and slaves from everywhere. You could buy almost anything in Ostia... at a price.

Coins were used all over the Empire to pay for goods. They had the Emperor's head stamped on one side. But there were no fixed prices. You needed to keep your bargaining skills razor sharp.

You could borrow money from a banker in the market place. But you might be sold into slavery if you couldn't pay back your debt.

TOP TIPS FOR TRAVELERS

1. ALWAYS CONSULT A SOOTHSAYER BEFORE YOU TRAVEL (SEE PAGE XIV).

2. AND MAKE AN OFFERING TO NEPTUNE, GOD OF THE SEA.

3. SAIL CLOSE TO THE COAST TO KEEP CLEAR OF PIRATES. (AND TO KEEP ON COURSE — COMPASSES HAVEN'T BEEN INVENTED YET.)

4. DON'T FORGET YOUR CLOAK — IT GETS NIPPY AT SEA.

5. NEVER TRAVEL ALONE (BY LAND OR SEA).

6. DON'T TRAVEL IN WINTER — THE WEATHER'S TERRIBLE AND YOU'RE BOUND TO GET SEASICK!

THE DAILY ROMAN
HOROSCOPE PAGE

PISCES FEB 19 - MARCH 20
MYSTIC MARCUS SAYS:
A GOOD WEEK FOR PISCEANS.
YOU'LL BE TOP OF YOUR CLASS
AND GET A RAISE IN YOUR
ALLOWANCE (NAG YOUR
PARENTS IF YOU DON'T).
YOU MAY SOON BE OFF ON A
LONG JOURNEY.
VII IS YOUR LUCKY NUMBER.

DID YOU KNOW?

You could always find work as a curse writer. To put a curse on someone, the Romans had the curse engraved on a stone tablet. This was then buried or thrown into a river. Thieves falling sick, villas falling down, and chariots losing their wheels were among the most popular curses.

THE ROMANS were extremely superstitious. They wouldn't do anything without consulting the gods or a soothsayer (fortuneteller). Telling the future was big business. As a soothsayer, you'd be in great demand. (As long as you didn't get it wrong!)

JOB DESCRIPTION: A JOB WITH A FUTURE. MUST BE GOOD WITH PEOPLE.

PAY: VARIES. DEPENDS HOW GOOD YOUR PREDICTIONS ARE.

THERE WERE MANY TYPES OF FORTUNE TELLERS:

1. A HARUSPEX WAS A PRIEST WHO TOLD THE WILL OF THE GODS BY LOOKING AT DEAD ANIMALS' INNARDS. NOT FOR YOU IF YOU'RE SQUEAMISH.

2. THE AUGURS WERE 16 PRIESTS WHO TOLD THE FUTURE BY LOOKING FOR SIGNS IN THE SKY, SUCH AS CLOUDS, LIGHTNING, HOW THE BIRDS FLEW, AND SO ON. SOUNDS TRICKY BUT TRAINING WAS GIVEN AT A COLLEGE IN ROME.

3. THE SIBYL WAS A SET OF BOOKS WRITTEN BY AN ANCIENT PROPHETESS. THEY WERE CONSULTED IN TIMES OF NATIONAL CRISIS, SUCH AS FAMINE OR PLAGUE.

4. ASTROLOGERS PREDICTED THE FUTURE FROM THE POSITION OF THE STARS AT A PERSON'S BIRTH. EVEN THE EMPERORS WOULD CONSULT THEM.

5. THE WAY THE SACRED CHICKENS PECKED THEIR CORN SHOWED WHETHER THE GODS APPROVED OF A PLAN OR NOT.

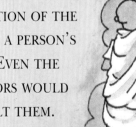

LUCKY GUIDELINES FOR AVOIDING DISASTER:

1. ALWAYS CONSULT A SOOTHSAYER BEFORE A JOURNEY. ONLY SET OUT IF YOU ARE TOLD IT'S SAFE TO TRAVEL.
2. TRY NOT TO SNEEZE. IT'S BAD LUCK.
3. IF YOU HEAR SOMETHING UNLUCKY, SPIT THREE TIMES TO GET RID OF THE BAD LUCK.
4. WHEN YOU'RE LEAVING THE HOUSE, NEVER TOUCH THE DOORSTEP WITH YOUR LEFT FOOT.
5. ONLY CUT YOUR HAIR WHEN THERE'S A FULL MOON.
6. NEVER LEAVE HOME WITHOUT YOUR BULLA (LUCKY CHARM).

STAR FILE

NAME: DIOCLES
TEAM: REDS
VICTORIES: 4,462
HEIGHT: 5 FEET 11 INCHES
HAIR: BROWN
EYES: BLUE
DATE OF BIRTH: AUGUST 1 100AD
STAR SIGN: LEO
HOBBIES: DIOCLES LIKES ANIMALS, TRAVELING AT SPEED AND MEETING PEOPLE.

THE STARTER DROPS HIS WHITE FLAG, there's a screech of wheels, a great cloud of dust, gasps from the crowd, and they're off... Chariot racing was hugely popular in Ancient Rome and people flocked to the Circus Maximus to watch the stars in action. A race lasted for seven thrilling laps of the track. The first past the post was the winner.

A quarter of a million people could fit into the Circus Maximus. What a noise!

Driving a chariot was dangerous work. It took a great deal of daring and skill. Many drivers were badly injured or even killed during a race. But it was worth it if you won. Successful charioteers became rich and famous superstars, got mobbed wherever they went, and were adored by fans.

The prize for the winner was a purse full of money and a victory crown.

JOB DESCRIPTION: GLAMOR, DANGER, AND SKILL ROLLED INTO ONE. POP STAR STATUS.

PAY: MILLIONS PAID FOR A WINNING STREAK.

Going to the races was a bit like going to a football match today, complete with stars, fans, and hooligans. There were four teams – the Reds, Greens, Whites, and Blues – each with their own band of supporters. The fans cheered and shouted their team on and placed bets on who would win. If the wrong team won, riots sometimes broke out among the crowd.

Some chariots had two horses. Most had four. The drivers wore no protection at all.

DID YOU KNOW?

As cars, planes, and trains had not been invented yet, Roman children would play with toy chariots and compete with each other for superstardom.

The most dangerous part of the race was hurtling round the tight bends. It took great strength and skill to keep control of the horses.

YOUNG CREATIVE PEOPLE
REQUIRED TO WORK IN BUSY
CRAFT SHOP.

APPLY TO CAIUS AT THE
LITTLE CRAFT SHOP IN
TRAJAN'S MARKET.

IF YOUR FATHER WAS A ROMAN CRAFTSMAN, the chances were you'd become one too. Most craftworkers had shops in town. They worked in the back, selling what they made from a counter at the front. You'd have spent many years here learning your craft.

MOSAIC MAKER

One of the most skillful craftsmen was the mosaic maker. Wealthy Romans loved to cover their villa floors with beautiful, and costly, mosaics. Here's how a mosaic was made:

1. The mosaic maker draws up a plan and if this is approved, he cuts the stones.

2. The floor is covered in wet plaster.

Mosaics are pictures made of tiny pieces of glass and stone.

DID YOU KNOW?

The Romans used polished metal for mirrors. Special mirror glass had not quite been invented yet.

3. The stones are pressed into the plaster, following the plan.

4. Finally, the mosaic is smoothed and polished.

WHO'S WHO IN ARTS AND CRAFTS

1. FRESCO PAINTER

FRESCOES ARE PICTURES PAINTED ON WET PLASTER. THE PLASTER HAS TO BE SMOOTH AND EVEN — IT TAKES A STEADY HAND!

2. BONE WORKER

THE ROMANS USE BONES FROM THE BUTCHERS TO MAKE COMBS, SWORD HILTS, AND KNIFE HANDLES.

3. SANDAL MAKER

SANDALS ARE MADE OF LEATHER OR CLOTH. SENATORS WEAR LEATHER BOOTS WITH A CRESCENT SHAPE ON THE TOE.

4. METALSMITH

WORKING WITH MANY METALS, METALSMITHS MAKE TOOLS, POTS, PANS, WEAPONS, AND JEWELRY.

5. GLASS BLOWER

GLASS IS BLOWN INTO BUBBLES FOR SHAPING INTO BOTTLES AND FLASKS.

6. CAMEO CARVER

CAMEOS ARE MINI CARVINGS OF PEOPLE OR ANIMALS, MADE FROM SEMIPRECIOUS STONE. THEY ARE WORN AS RINGS OR BROOCHES.

7. POTTER

POTTERS MAKE WINE CUPS AND CROCKERY. SOME WORK IN FACTORIES AND CHURN OUT POTS BY THE MILLION.

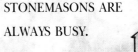

8. STONEMASON

WORKING ON TEMPLES, BUILDINGS, ARCHES, AND EVEN GRAVESTONES, STONEMASONS ARE ALWAYS BUSY.

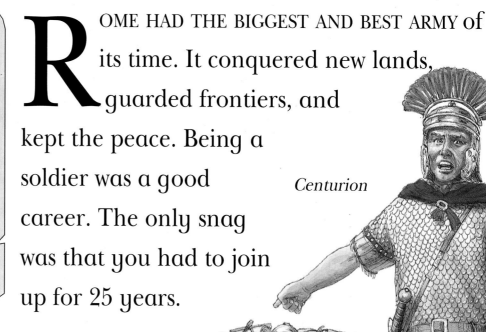

Centurion

THE DAILY ROMAN
ARMY • CAREERS • SERVICE

DO YOU...
... ENJOY A CHALLENGE?
... LIKE EXERCISE?
... LOOK GOOD IN UNIFORM?
... WANT TO SEE THE WORLD AND MEET INTERESTING PEOPLE?
...WANT A CAREER FOR LIFE?
IF SO...
... WHY NOT JOIN THE ARMY?

FOR AN APPLICATION FORM, CONTACT CENTURION QUINTUS SEXTUS AT THE BARRACKS.

ROME HAD THE BIGGEST AND BEST ARMY of its time. It conquered new lands, guarded frontiers, and kept the peace. Being a soldier was a good career. The only snag was that you had to join up for 25 years.

A legion was made up of about 5,000 soldiers. They were divided into smaller units of 80 men, called a century.

LIFE IN THE ARMY

1. You join the army as a legionary and go off to camp.

2. You swear loyalty to the Emperor.

3. You are measured for your uniform.

4. Training begins. You practice fighting, learn to ride, swim, pitch camp...

JOB DESCRIPTION: STEADY JOB WITH REGULAR INCOME. MINIMUM SERVICE 25 YEARS. CHANCES FOR PROMOTION.

PAY: GOOD, WITH PENSION ON RETIREMENT.

YOUR UNIFORM

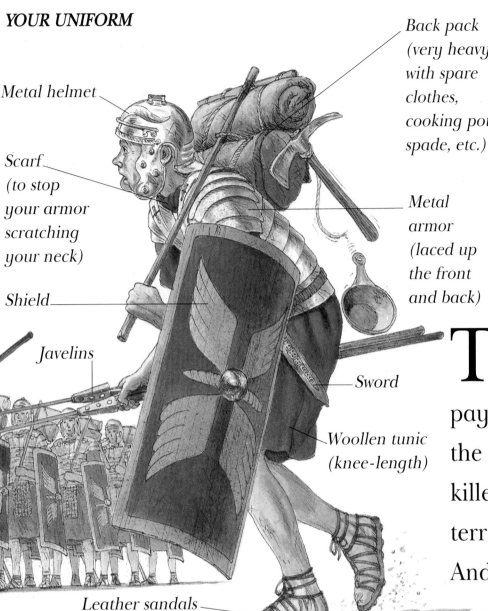

Metal helmet

Scarf (to stop your armor scratching your neck)

Shield

Javelins

Leather sandals (studded with nails)

Back pack (very heavy! with spare clothes, cooking pot, spade, etc.)

Metal armor (laced up the front and back)

Sword

Woollen tunic (knee-length)

DID YOU KNOW?
Roman soldiers had to pay for their food. The word "salary" comes from the Latin for "salt-money."

The army offered a steady job and regular pay. Of course, you also ran the risk of being wounded or killed in battle. The food was terrible and strictly rationed. And all that marching really made your feet ache!

5. ... and march for miles. Very hard work!

6. At last, a real battle. You come through with flying colors and return in triumph. You'll be a centurion (in charge of a century) before you know it!

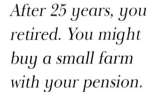

After 25 years, you retired. You might buy a small farm with your pension.

L EARNING TO FIGHT was not the only reason for joining the army. It also gave you the chance to learn other skills, such as building or engineering. To keep you busy between battles, you were set to work building roads. Not a popular job but someone had to do it.

DID YOU KNOW?

Each mile was marked by a milestone. (A Roman mile was 1,000 paces long.) The milestone gave the distances from the towns where the road started and finished. It also showed the name of the Emperor whose reign the road was built in.

BUILDING A ROMAN ROAD

1. The surveyor planned the shortest, straightest route for the road to take.

2. The soldiers set to work, digging a trench and filling it with layers of stone.(This is where you came in!)

LEGIONARIES

Your work didn't end with roads. There were still plenty of aqueducts, viaducts, bridges, basilicas, temples, amphitheaters, triumphal arches, and tombs to build which needed a helping hand. Luckily arches and concrete had been invented to make your life easier. There were also thousands of slaves to do most of the dirtiest work!

3. Then you laid paving stones on top.

4. The road had a curved surface so the rain could drain away.

Aqueducts were bridges that carried water to towns and cities.

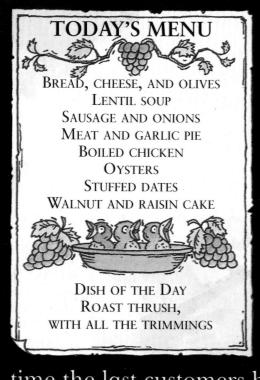

TODAY'S MENU

BREAD, CHEESE, AND OLIVES
LENTIL SOUP
SAUSAGE AND ONIONS
MEAT AND GARLIC PIE
BOILED CHICKEN
OYSTERS
STUFFED DATES
WALNUT AND RAISIN CAKE

DISH OF THE DAY
ROAST THRUSH,
WITH ALL THE TRIMMINGS

MEET DIDIUS. He's the owner of the Jolly Roman, a popular inn near the Forum. Apart from wine, he does a sideline in good pub grub. He works very long hours, getting up early to serve his first hungry customers with breakfast. And it's late at night by the time the last customers have gone home.

There were many inns and hot-food stalls lining the streets. Each had an L-shaped, marble counter with huge stone jars sunk into it. They were used for keeping food hot and for storing wine. You could eat in or carry out – or even stay the night in a guest room above the bar.

JOB DESCRIPTION: FAMILY-RUN BUSINESS WITH MANY REGULAR CUSTOMERS. ACCOMMODATION ABOVE SHOP.

PAY: GOOD, IF YOU DON'T EAT OR DRINK ALL THE PROFITS.

If you were poor in Ancient Rome, you probably lived in a cramped, crowded block of flats with no proper kitchen to cook in. Instead, you walked over to the local carryout for dinner!

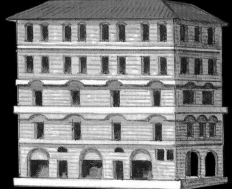

There was no tea or coffee in Ancient Rome. Wine was the usual drink. This was watered down – it was rude to drink it neat! Or it was mixed with sweet honey or spices and drunk warm from pottery wine cups.

DID YOU KNOW?

Roman flats had no running water. You had to fetch supplies from public fountains in the street. Not much fun if you lived on the fifth floor!

There were so many brawls in the inns that the Emperor tried to close them down!

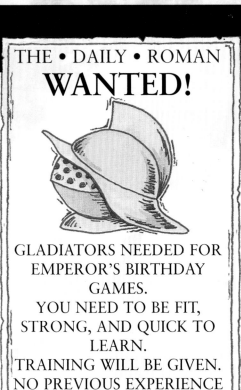

MOST ROMAN GLADIATORS were prisoners of war, slaves, or condemned criminals. There were even some women. You only applied for this job if you were really down on your luck. Being a gladiator wasn't a very long or secure career. You were trained in a special school, then expected to fight to the death.

Some gladiators carry a sword, a small shield, and a heavy bronze helmet. If they die, their armor is handed down to other gladiators.

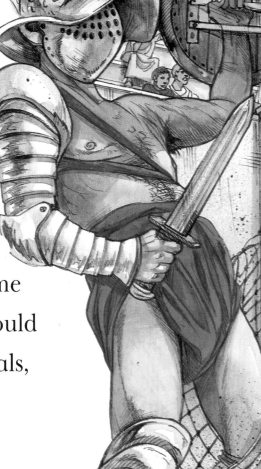

The Ancient Romans loved gladiator fights – the more blood and gore, the better. They cheered their heroes' every move and booed losers or cowards. Some gladiators fought one-on-one and some in groups. Other fighters would face wild animals, such as leopards.

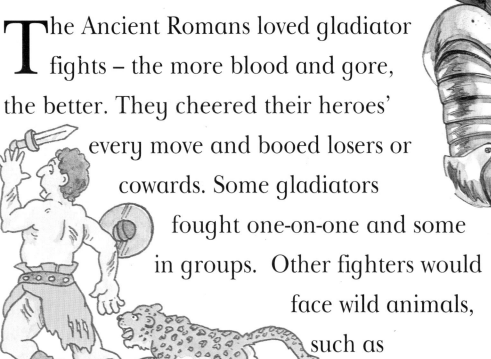

Some gladiators were treated like film stars. But their glamorous lives were often short. If you were very brave (and very lucky), you might survive. You were given a wooden sword, called a rudis, a crown, a small fortune, and your freedom. Many freed fighters became gladiator trainers.

Others have a net to catch the opponent and a giant fork, called a trident, to stab him with. They have to be quick on their feet.

Sometimes a spear may be a gladiator's only weapon.

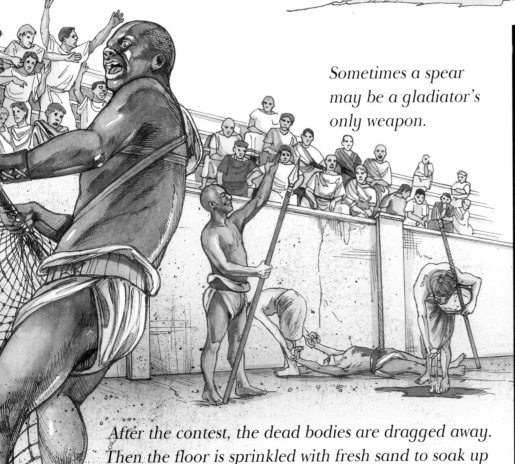

DID YOU KNOW?
The loser is at the mercy of the crowd. A "thumbs up" sign means he lives. "Thumbs down" means certain death.

After the contest, the dead bodies are dragged away. Then the floor is sprinkled with fresh sand to soak up the blood and with incense to hide the smell!

WITHOUT MILLIONS OF SLAVES doing all the hardest and dirtiest jobs, the Roman Empire would have ground to a halt. If your parents were slaves, you'd be a slave too. Other slaves were prisoners of war, sold to the highest bidder at a slave market. You were owned by a wealthy Roman or by the government, and your whole life was at their beck and call. You had no freedom and no rights at all.

Your fate depended on whether your owner was a slave driver or a softie. Many slaves were cruelly treated. A lucky few were well looked after and even paid wages. If they saved enough money, they could buy their freedom.

Slaves had to wear tags with their masters' names on.

JOB DESCRIPTION: LOWEST OF THE LOW. ON DUTY 24 HOURS A DAY. GRIM FUTURE.

PAY: NONE. OPTIONAL LOYALTY BONUS.

A buyer might consider carefully before choosing a slave.

TEN USES FOR A ROMAN SLAVE

1. WORKING IN THE MINES. A FATE WORSE THAN DEATH.

2. DOING YOUR MISTRESS'S HAIR AND MAKE-UP.

3. PICKING GRAPES AND MAKING WINE ON A COUNTRY ESTATE.

4. BUILDING A TEMPLE. A JOB FOR GOVERNMENT-OWNED SLAVES.

5. DIGGING GRAVES. ANOTHER JOB FOR GOVERNMENT SLAVES.

6. GUARDING YOUR MASTER'S CLOTHES AT THE BATHS.

7. SINGING AND DANCING AT BANQUETS AND PARADES.

8. WIPING GUESTS' HANDS BETWEEN COURSES AT BANQUETS.

9. TEACHING THE CHILDREN OF WEALTHY ROMANS. FOR EDUCATED GREEK SLAVES ONLY.

10. WORKING IN THE CIVIL SERVICE, ADVISING THE EMPEROR. NOT MANY SLAVES MADE IT THIS FAR.

DID YOU KNOW?

Slaves weren't allowed to watch gladiator fights. But many ended up in the ring as gladiators!

FREE TICKETS TO THE GLADIATOR FIGHTS

GLADIATOR TRAINEES

GLOSSARY

Amphitheater

A circular open-air building with seats arranged in tiers.

Augustus

The first Emperor of Rome. He ruled from 27BC-AD14. He brought peace and prosperity to Rome after years of war and unrest.

Basilica

A large public building used as a law court. It sometimes contained shops and offices.

Caligula

Emperor of Rome from AD37-41. His real name was Gaius. He was murdered after ruling for just four years.

Centurion

A Roman soldier in charge of a "century," consisting of about 80 legionaries.

Circus Maximus

The racetrack in Rome, used for chariot racing.

Claudius

He became Emperor after Caligula and ruled from AD41-54. He was very intelligent and ruled wisely and well.

Colosseum

The biggest Roman amphitheater which could seat 50,000 people. You can still visit it in Rome today.

Diocles

A superstar charioteer who was born in AD100. He rode for the Red team and racked up an astonishing 4,462 victories.

Engineer

A person who designed and organized the building of roads, bridges, viaducts and aqueducts.

Forum

The market place in Rome.

Javelin

A light spear that was thrown by hand. Roman soldiers would carry two of them.

Nero

Emperor of Rome from AD54-68. He was a cruel tyrant who murdered anyone who crossed him (including his mother). He was eventually forced to leave Rome and later killed himself.

Pension

A sum of money given to Roman soldiers when they had completed their 25 years of service.

Roman Empire

The territories governed by Rome.

Senator

A Roman politician. He was a member of the Senate that ruled Rome under the Emperor.

Toga

The loose, flowing wrap worn by men in Rome.

Treason

An act of betrayal or disloyalty to the Emperor, punishable by death.

Tyrant

A cruel and unjust ruler or master.

Viaduct

A bridge that carries roads over rivers and valleys.

GETTING PAID
If you were lucky enough to be paid for your job (and not everyone was!) you might have received coins like these. They were made from gold, silver, bronze or copper and had the Emperor's head stamped on them.

INDEX

1 I		17 XVII	
2 II		18 XVIII	
3 III		19 XIX	
4 IV		20 XX	
5 V		21 XXI	
6 VI		22 XXII	
7 VII		23 XXIII	
8 VIII		24 XXIV	
9 IX		25 XXV	
10 X		26 XXVI	
11 XI		27 XXVII	
12 XII		28 XXVIII	
13 XIII		29 XXIX	
14 XIV		30 XXX	
15 XV		31 XXXI	
16 XVI		32 XXXII